YOUR KNOWLEDGE HAS VALUE

AF153583

- We will publish your bachelor's and
  master's thesis, essays and papers

- Your own eBook and book -
  sold worldwide in all relevant shops

- Earn money with each sale

Upload your text at www.GRIN.com
and publish for free

Business Research Methodology. An Introductory Guide for Business Scholars

Dr. David E. Amanawa

Bibliographic information published by the German National Library:

The German National Library lists this publication in the National Bibliography; detailed bibliographic data are available on the Internet at http://dnb.dnb.de.

ISBN: 9783389004463
This book is also available as an ebook.

© GRIN Publishing GmbH
Trappentreustraße 1
80339 München

All rights reserved

Print and binding: Books on Demand GmbH, Norderstedt, Germany
Printed on acid-free paper from responsible sources.

The present work has been carefully prepared. Nevertheless, authors and publishers do not incur liability for the correctness of information, notes, links and advice as well as any printing errors.

GRIN web shop: https://www.grin.com/document/1448747

IGNATIUS AJURU UNIVERSITY OF EDUCATION

Course Title:

BUSINESS RESEARCH METHODOLOGY

Course Lecturer

DR. DAVID E. AMANAWA

INTRODUCTION

The term "research" is derived from the old French word "recerchier," which means to search and search again. It means to repeat a search for something, and it suggests that the previous search was not thorough and complete in the sense that there is still room for improvement. In common usage, research refers to the pursuit of knowledge. It is a methodical and systematic search for relevant information on a given topic or region. In truth, research is a scientific inquiry art. According to the Advanced Learner's Dictionary of Current English, research is "a careful investigation or inquiry, especially through the search for new facts in any branch of knowledge." Research is also a systematic effort to gain new knowledge. Some individuals regard research as moving from the known to the unknown. It is, in fact, a trip of discovery.

Research is a scientific strategy for answering a research question, solving a problem, or developing new knowledge by collecting, organizing, and analyzing information systems to make the research helpful in decision-making. Systematic investigation in any field. Three fundamental operations are involved in the realm of investigation:

1. Data collection: It refers to observing, measuring, and recording information.
2. Data analysis refers to arranging and organizing the collected data to find out their significance and generalize about them.
3. Report writing: It is an inseparable part and an outcome of a research study. Its purpose is to convey the information contained in it to the readers or audience.

Research is an activity that leads us to new facts and information, assists us in validating current knowledge, and causes us to question things that are difficult to explain based on existing evidence. To be a great manager, you must understand how to make the appropriate judgments by understanding the numerous phases involved in finding solutions to challenging challenges. It can also be understood in the following terms:

- Research is a continual activity in the vast majority of subjects and professions.
- It aids in critically evaluating how we operate, implement policies, and issue directions in our professions.
- It is the systematic observation of processes to find better methods to do things, decrease the work required to attain an aim and determine the validity of the targets.
- In truth, research is a subconscious activity that we constantly engage in, whether purchasing daily use items, a car, an electronic device, or arranging a vacation.

CHARACTERISTICS OF RESEARCH

Research is a process in which we strive to answer a question, solve a problem, or get a better knowledge of phenomena in a methodical and data-supported manner. This procedure contains seven different features:

1. It all begins with a query or an issue.
2. An explicit aim must be articulated.
3. Follows a specified procedural strategy.
4. Usually breaks the main difficulty into smaller, more manageable sub-problems.
5. The study challenge, query, or hypothesis directs it.
6. Certain fundamental assumptions are accepted.
7. Data collection and analysis are required in order to tackle the problem that prompted the research.

The primary goal or purpose of research in any field of study is to contribute to what is known about the topic under examination by employing scientific procedures. Listed below are the research's objectives, which could be either; explorative, descriptive, predictive, or casually explanative.

Explorative: Exploration is the discovery of previously unknown phenomena. It is essential when researchers are unsure of the challenges they may face throughout the investigation. In addition, researchers can develop notions more clearly via investigation; priorities must be established. Exploratory studies have flexible frameworks with the goal of uncovering future research projects.

Descriptive: The term descriptive refers to data-driven information-collecting operations. Descriptive studies are those that describe conditions and happenings via research. Descriptive studies address the questions of who, what, when, where, and how.

Predictive: Prediction aims to explain when and under what circumstances the event will occur, assuming a reasonable explanation can be supplied for the vent in question. It will be able to forecast when an event will occur and explain it after it has occurred.

Casually Explanative: Explanatory research goes beyond description to establish a cause-and-effect link between variables. It explains why the phenomena described in the research occurred. Thus, if a researcher discovers that communities with larger family sizes have more significant child mortality, he or she is doing a descriptive study. An explanatory study is conducted when a researcher explains why something is the way it is and attempts to show a cause-and-effect link.

PURPOSE OF RESEARCH

A specific research project's purpose may fall into one of the two major categories listed below.

- Become acquainted with phenomena or gain fresh insights about them.
- Accurately portray the qualities of a specific individual, circumstance, or group.
- Determine the frequency with which something happens or is connected.
- Examine the causal link between two or more facts or circumstances.
- Know and comprehend a phenomenon in order to correctly formulate a problem.

- Accurately describe a particular phenomenon and test theories concerning correlations between its various characteristics.

Some more research aims are: Provide answers to complicated issues; investigate natural laws; make fresh discoveries; develop new goods; save money; improve our lives; and human wants.

UNDERSTANDING RESEARCH TOPICS

A research topic is a subject or issue a researcher is particularly interested in when conducting a study. Every effective research effort begins with a well-defined study subject. The process of selecting a subject is ongoing, in which scholars investigate, clarify, and develop their ideas (Allen, 2017). There are a few things to consider when choosing a topic; let us see a few below:

Discover your Interests: Your interests should be a top consideration when selecting a study topic. Since you must devote much time to studying and writing about the subject, you must be enthusiastic about it. Make a list of suitable study subjects based on your interests, pastimes, or areas of specialization to get started. You may also think about the subjects that stuck out to you in your readings or the courses that you have loved the most.

Review other Literature: Before choosing a study topic, you must know the existing literature. You can detect knowledge gaps, discrepancies in results, or open-ended questions that you can further investigate by preliminary assessing the literature already published on your subject. Reading scholarly works, novels, and other pertinent materials in your profession will help you do this. Take note of any themes or subjects that surface, and then use this knowledge to determine the direction of your research question.

Seek advice from your Supervisor: You can get insightful advice on selecting a research subject from your academic adviser (project supervisor) or a professional mentor. They can offer advice on new research topics, recommend areas of interest, and evaluate the viability of your research plan. Additionally, they may point you toward pertinent books and other materials that can aid in advancing your study.

Examine the Potentials and Viability: The study topic you select should be manageable within the limitations of your project's time and budget allocation. Make sure you are not attempting to handle a topic that is too wide or too narrow by being careful of the breadth of your study. If your topic is too broad, it could be challenging to perform a thorough analysis. If it is too limited, you might have trouble finding adequate sources to back up your study.

Have Discussions with peers: You might come up with fresh ideas and viewpoints by talking with your friends or coworkers about prospective study subjects. They could have knowledge or insight you had not thought about, and their comments might help you improve your study topic. In order to connect with other researchers and get inspiration for your study, you may also join academic organizations or go to conferences in your field.

Think about the Relevance: Select a study area that is pertinent to your field of study and has the potential to further your understanding. To choose themes that are both pertinent and fascinating, take into account the most recent developments and hot topics in your industry. It is also more likely that your study will be published or presented at conferences if it is on a current and essential topic.

Maintain a Flexible Mind: While picking a study topic that fits your interests and areas of experience is essential, you should also be open to investigating novel concepts or subjects outside your comfort zone. Consider looking into a subject that contradicts your presumptions or offers fresh viewpoints you had not thought about. You could find fresh viewpoints or insights that help improve your research and advance your research career.

ELEMENTS OF THE RESEARCH QUESTION

According to Hassan (2022), a research topic often consists of some elements that aid in defining and clarifying the research project's subject matter. These elements consist of:

- This research problem represents the main topic or inquiry the research seeks to answer. Therefore, it must have boundaries that identify its scope and keep the study narrow.
- Background and context: This section gives the study topic the relevant background knowledge and context. It justifies the significance, applicability, and timeliness of the study subject or question. A literature review that describes the prior investigation into the subject may also be included.
- Objectives or aims: This section describes the precise objectives or goals the study tries to accomplish. It must be accurate, succinct, and pertinent to the study topic or subject.
- Methodology: This section outlines the procedures and tools that will be utilized to gather and examine the data. It should include information on the sampling strategy, data collecting methods, and statistical analyses in sufficient depth to provide readers with a clear picture of how the study will be conducted.
- Contribution or significance: This section describes the importance or relevance of the study topic. It should show how the study will advance the knowledge in the area and how practitioners, decision-makers, or society will gain from it.
- Limits: This section describes the research's restrictions, including potential biases, presumptions, or limits. It should be open and truthful about any potential flaws in the study and how these issues will be resolved.
- Expected results or findings: This section summarizes the research project's anticipated results or findings. It needs to be grounded in the goals and methods of the study and feasible.

Finding a specific area of study to examine and investigate is the goal of choosing a research topic. The majority of the time, a research subject is a broad area of interest that has to be further explored and refined during the research process. It aids in defining the research questions and objectives and gives the study a defined focus and direction. A well-defined research subject also ensures that the study is pertinent, helpful, and able to add to the body of knowledge already in the area. Ultimately, a study topic aims to provide fresh perceptions, information, and comprehension of certain phenomena, concerns, or issues.

BUSINESS RESEARCH

(Kabir, 2018) describes business research as the methodical and objective process of gathering data for corporate decision-making. Business research should be impartial; thus, the data collected should be neutral and detached rather than prejudiced. The management decision-making process is aided by research in many facets of a firm. It reduces the likelihood of making bad judgments by reducing decision ambiguity. Research should support management decision-making, not take its place. He further explained that the scope of business research covers the following aspects:

Production Management: Research is crucial in creating new products, product diversification, product introduction, product enhancement, process technologies, site selection, and new investment.

Personnel Management: Research is helpful for organizational growth, motivating strategy formulation, job redesign, and organizational restructuring.

Marketing Management: Research plays a significant role in determining the target market's size and composition, as well as customer behavior in terms of attitudes, lifestyle, and influences. It is the main instrument for deciding on price policy, choosing a distribution channel, and developing sales strategies, product mixes, and promotional plans.

Financial Management: Research may help manage a portfolio, paying out dividends, raising cash, hedging against currency swings, and keeping track of product cycles.

Materials management: It is used to decide which supplier to use, to decide whether to create or buy something, and to decide on negotiating tactics.

General Management: It makes a significant contribution to the creation of standards, objectives, long-term objectives, and growth plans.

You must possess an awareness of scientific methodologies and the ability to incorporate them into decision-making in order to function successfully in a complicated context. You'll need to comprehend what constitutes quality research and how to do it. The quantity and capability of the tools available to do research have increased in tandem with the corporate environment's increased complexity.

STAGES OF THE RESEARCH

The research project can be separated into three phases: planning, project, and documentation (Kabir, 2018).

Phase of Planning: One of the keys to producing a good study is meticulous planning from the start. A proposal is the project planning procedure. A proposal's purpose is to address four questions: (a) What steps will be taken? (c) Why is it vital to do this? (c) What are the work's objectives and scope? and (d) how will it be accomplished?

Project Phase: The project phase refers to the actual work on the project. Keeping a journal or project record during the period is an excellent idea. It is a time to reflect on what has been accomplished as well as look forward to what needs to be accomplished. It is also helpful to sometimes put up preliminary explanations of what has been done to aid later in the documentation process.

Documentation Phase: The documentation phase, or research preparation, should continue continuously throughout the project. Much of the final document can be based on the proposal and progress updates prepared throughout the project phase.

A general outline for a research report is shown below. Of course, the demands of the project may necessitate deviating from this plan.

Table 1: Documentation Phases of Project Writing

Beginning Material:	Cover Page, Title Page, Abstract, Keyword list, Table of Contents, List of Figures and Tables, Acknowledgements
Chapter 1:	Introduction – Statement of the Problem, Hypotheses, Why it is Important, Objectives of the Work, Scope of the Work
Chapter 2:	Background and Literature Review – Discuss related work and indicate how it relates to report
Chapter 3:	Methodology – Describe the procedure used in project, data used, and how it was obtained
Chapter 4:	Results – Indicate what happened and interpret what it means
Chapter 5:	Conclusions and Recommendations – Summarize conclusions and what they mean (i.e., answer the question, "So what?"). What changes and further work do you recommend?

Source: (Kabir, 2018)

Every study project always starts with a topic or a problem of some kind. Through the use of scientific methods, research seeks to learn "more" about "something" or to find the answers to important questions. This general research rule does not apply to legal research. However, conducting and carrying out legal research as a methodical investigation is a difficult procedure.

There are three stages to the procedure. Each of them calls for talent. The steps are designing the research (Planning Phase), carrying it out (Project Phase), and disseminating the results (Documentation Phase).

The requisite sub-skills for fact gathering, legal analysis, legal knowledge, problem identification, legal analysis, fact analysis, additional fact collecting, identification of research paths, and production of key (search) words are required for research planning. The skills related to problem-solving, finding relevant research materials, finding those materials, using them effectively, analysing research findings, applying those findings to the problems that have been identified, and finding new problems are all part of the second-stage processes of research implementation. While the third stage of the process, which is the presentation of research findings, calls for the abilities needed to: identify the needs of the (research) recipients; choose an appropriate format or framework; use clear and succinct language; and use an appropriate language-style (informative, advisory, recommendatory, or demanding) (Kabir, 2018).

Cover Page

The first official page of an essay or paper is the cover page. It serves to lend a professional perspective to a report, academic dissertation, or thesis. It's the first thing a teacher or lecturer notices when they get a piece of work. Typically, it includes details like the author's name, essay title, course name and code, affiliation with the author's university, and so on (Indeed, 2022).

Title Page

Since the title page is the opening page of your project, it's critical to have a properly structured title page that accurately summarises the whole work. Everything a reader needs to know about the article's contents, authors, place of origin, and article category should be included on this page (Enago, 2021).

Abstract

An abstract is a succinct synopsis of your work that is typically one paragraph in length (6-7 sentences, 150–250 words). An effective abstract does several things (Madison, 2023):

An abstract prepares readers to follow the detailed information, analyses, and arguments in your full paper; it enables readers to quickly grasp the gist or essence of your paper or article; and, later, it aids readers in remembering key points from your paper.

It's important to keep in mind that search engines and bibliographic databases find essential phrases for indexing published papers using abstracts in addition to titles. Therefore, the information you provide in your title and abstract will be vital in assisting other scholars in finding your paper or article.

Table of Contents

The chapters and significant portions of your thesis, dissertation, or research paper should be listed in the table of contents together with their corresponding page numbers. An effective table of contents sets the tone for the rest of your work by showing your reader that it will be of the highest calibre. The table of contents (TOC) ought to come after the introduction and before the abstract. Two pages should be the absolute limit. There are several formatting alternatives available for your thesis, paper, or dissertation, depending on the nature of the subject (George, Dissertation Table of Contents in Word | Instructions & Examples, 2022).

Aknowledgement

You have the chance to express your gratitude to those who have supported you both personally and professionally throughout the writing of your thesis or dissertation in the acknowledgements section. The acknowledgements section of your thesis or dissertation, which appears between your title page and abstract, shouldn't be more than one page long. You may use first-person pronouns and a less formal writing style than is often accepted in academic writing in your acknowledgements. In contrast to the academic work itself, acknowledgements are your opportunity to express something more intimate (George, 2022).

Chapter 1: Introduction

This chapter outlines the thesis' research strategy and gives a general summary of the research that is described in it. The context and goals of this research are discussed at the beginning of the chapter. The relevance of the research and its goals are then covered in the next section of the chapter. The importance of user competency and self-efficacy is then emphasised. The research questions and hypotheses come next. The discussion of the analytical unit follows. The study's research design, cultural influence, and research setting are then described. The preliminary research model is then presented in this chapter. Each of the five chapters of this thesis is briefly described in the thesis outline.

Chapter 2: Literature Review

The findings of the relevant literature are presented in this chapter. The literature review discussed here assesses earlier work to give a context on the important ideas investigated in this study. There are eight (8) primary goals for the literature review:

1. To identify issues and "gaps" in the existing literature.
2. To identify issues and help the candidate determine and articulate their current level of knowledge.
3. To identify where additional research is needed, to introduce theory that is usefully related to the explanation of the key constructs.
4. To help the candidate identify the salient characteristics of expertise.

5. To develop candidate's research skills, to conduct environmental scans, to read selectively.
6. To develop candidate's skills of critical appraisal and your capacity to recognise the objectives and arguments of those you are reading, and to articulate their strengths and weaknesses.
7. To think laterally and creatively about potential research areas.
8. To serve as a source of explanation for phenomena observed in model and hypotheses testing.

Chapter 3: Research Methodology

Another important component of the research project writing is chapter three, which discusses the study process. You describe the aim of the study, the approach you plan to take, the tools you'll use, where you'll gather your data, the categories of data you'll be gathering, and how you'll gather it in chapter three of your research project. It describes the many techniques that will be employed in the research endeavour. Here, you describe the methods and tactics you'll use for the study, such as the research design, study design in research, research area (the study's focus), and study population. You also explain to the reader your study design procedures, the rationale behind your technique selection, your analytic procedure, and how you intended to analyse your data. You should write your approach in clear, basic language so that other researchers may use it and get the same conclusions or results.

When you want to conduct research on a specific area or behaviour using tools like structured questionnaires or interviews, or if you want to manipulate some variables, you can choose a survey design.

Chapter 4: Results

It describes the many techniques that will be employed in the research endeavour. Here, you describe the methods and tactics you'll use for the study, such as the research design, study design in research, research area (the study's focus), and study population. You also explain to the reader your study design procedures, the rationale behind your technique selection, your analytic procedure, and how you intended to analyse your data. You should write your approach in clear, basic language so that other researchers may use it and get the same conclusions or results.

When you want to conduct research on a specific area or behaviour using tools like structured questionnaires or interviews, or if you want to manipulate some variables, you can choose a survey design.

Chapter 5: Conclusions, Limitations and Reccommendations

The research-related works are compiled in this chapter, together with potential contributions, restrictions, and recommendations for further research. It starts out with an overview of the study before talking about how generalizable the results are. A review of the key consequences for both research and practise is then included.

After that, the research's weaknesses are listed and potential future research possibilities are discussed. The section on future research outlines further relevant research concerns that may be addressed with new methodologies and fresh data as well as alternate techniques to support the conclusions of this study. This is followed by your recommendations for modifications and more effort.

APA Referencing Style (7th Edition)

The American Psychological Association governs the APA style, which is a writing norm accepted by the majority of institutions and Psychology publications across the world. It establishes a uniform method for writing and referencing psychological academic writings. This is based on the 7th version of the American Psychological Association's Publication Manual, which was released in 2020.

The figures below by (Columbia College, 2023) shows a brief summary and explanations on how to use the APA 7th edition:

Fig 1: About In-text Citations

About In-Text Citation

In APA, in-text citations are inserted in the body of your research paper to briefly document the source of your information. Brief in-text citations point the reader to more complete information in the reference list at the end of the paper.

- In-text citations include the last name of the author followed by a comma and the publication year enclosed in parentheses: (Smith, 2007).
- If you are quoting directly the page number should be included, if given. If you are paraphrasing the page number is not required.
- If the author's name is not given, then use the first word or words of the title. Follow the same formatting that was used in the title, such as italics: (*Naturopathic*, 2007).

Fig 2: How to Cite 2 or More works by same author with same year of publication

FAQ - How do I cite two or more works by the same author with the same year of publication?

When you are citing two different sources that share the same author and year of publication, assign lowercase letters after the year of publication (a, b, c, etc.). Assign these letters according to which title comes first alphabetically. Use these letters in both in-text citations and the Reference list.

Example In-Text:

Paraphrasing content from first source by this author (Daristotle, 2015a). "Now I am quoting from the second source by the same author" (Daristotle, 2015b, p. 50).

Example Reference List entries:

Daristotle, J. (2015a). *Name of book used as first source.* Toronto, ON: Fancy Publisher.

Daristotle, J. (2015b). *Title of book used as second source.* Toronto, ON: Very Fancy Publisher.

Fig 3: How to cite a work quoted in another source

FAQ - How do I cite a work quoted in another source?

Sometimes an author of a book, article or website will mention another person's work by using a quotation or paraphrased idea from that source. The work that is mentioned in the article you are reading is called the primary source. The article you are reading is called the secondary source.

For example, suppose you are reading an article by Brown (2014) that cites information from an article by Snow (1982) that you would like to include in your essay. For the reference list, you will only make a citation for the secondary source (Brown). You do not put in a citation for the primary source (Snow) in the reference list. For the in-text citation, you identify the primary source (Snow) and then write "as cited in" the secondary source (Brown). If you know the year of the publication of the primary source, include it in the in-text citation. Otherwise, you can omit it. See below for examples.

Examples of in-text citations:

According to a study by Snow (1982, as cited in Brown, 2014), 75% of students believe that teachers should not assign nightly homework.

Note: If you don't have the publication date of Snow's article, you just omit it like this:
According to a study by Snow (as cited in Brown, 2014), 75% of students believe that teachers should not assign nightly homework.

In fact, 75% of students believe that teachers should not assign nightly homework (Snow, 1982, as cited in Brown, 2014).

Snow (1982, as cited in Brown, 2014) concluded that "nightly homework is a great stressor for many students" (p.34).

Example of Reference list citation:

Brown, S. (2014). Trends in homework assignments. *Journal of Secondary Studies, 12(3),* 29-38. http://doi.org/fsfsbit

Fig 4: In-text Citation for 2 or more Authors

In-Text Citation For Two or More Authors/Editors

Number of Authors/Editors	First Time Paraphrased	Second and Subsequent Times Paraphrased
Two	(Case & Daristotle, 2011)	(Case & Daristotle, 2011)
Three or more	(Case et al., 2011)	(Case et al., 2011)

Fig 5: What's New in the 7th Edition of APA

What's New in the 7th Edition of APA?

Below is a summary of the major changes in the 7th edition of the APA Publication Manual.

Essay Format:

- Font - While you still can use Times New Roman 12, you are free to use other fonts. Calibri 11, Arial 11, Lucida Sans 10, and Georgia 11 are all acceptable.
- Headers - No running headers are required for student papers.
- Tables and Figures - There is a standardized format for both tables and figures.

Style, Grammar, Usage:

- Singular "they" required in two situations: when used by a known person as their personal pronoun or when the gender of a singular person is not known.
- Use only one space after a sentence-ending period.

Citation Style:

- Developed the 'Four Elements of a Reference" (Author, Date, Title, Source) to help writers to create references for source types not explicitly examined in the APA Manual.
- Three or more authors can be abbreviated to First author, et al. on the first citation.
- Up to 20 authors are spelled out in the References List.
- Publisher location is not required for books.
- Ebook platform, format, or device is not required for eBooks.
- Library database names are generally not required.
- **Hyperlinks** -
  - No "doi:" prefix, simply include the doi.
  - All hyperlinks retain the https://
  - Links can be "live" in blue with underline or black without underlining

CONCLUSION

All of the procedures utilised by the researcher to explore his or her research topic are referred to as research methods. The conduct and tools we use in executing research operations such as making observations, capturing data, data processing procedures, and so on are referred to as research techniques. The actions and equipment used in selecting and creating research procedures are referred to as research methods. Methods, on the other hand, are more generic. Techniques are generated by methods. In practise, however, the two phrases are used interchangeably, and when we refer of research methods, we implicitly include research procedures within their scope.

A research technique is a method for solving a research problem in a methodical manner. It may be thought of as a science that studies how scientific research is conducted. In it, we look at the many processes that a researcher takes to explore his or her research topic, as well as the reasoning behind them. The researcher must understand not only the research methods/techniques but also the methodology.

Researchers must not only understand how to create specific indices or tests, calculate the Mean, Mode, Median, standard deviation, or chi-square, and apply specific research techniques, but they must also understand which of these methods or techniques are relevant and which are not, and what they mean and indicate and why.

According to (Kabir, 2018); in order for the research results to be able to be evaluated by the researcher themselves as well as by outside parties, research methodology not only discusses the research methods but also takes into account the logic behind the methods we use in the context of our research study. When we discuss research methodology, the reasons for conducting a study, how the research problem was defined, how and why the hypothesis was developed, what data were collected, what particular method was used, why a particular technique for data analysis was used, and a host of other questions of a similar nature are typically addressed.

References

Allen, M. (2017). Research topic, definition of research methodology. *The Sage Encyclopedia of Communication Research Methods.*, https://doi.org/10.4135/9781483381411 .

Columbia College. (2023). *APA Citation Guide (7th edition) : Welcome.* Retrieved from Culumbia College, Vancouver, Canada: https://columbiacollege-ca.libguides.com/c.php?g=713274&p=5082913

Enago. (2021). *Writing the Title Page (Part 1).* Retrieved from Enago Academy: https://www.enago.com/academy/writing-title-page-part-1

George, T. (2022). *Dissertation Table of Contents in Word | Instructions & Examples.* Retrieved from Scribbr: https://www.scribbr.com/dissertation/table-of-contents/#:~:text=The%20table%20of%20contents%20is,paper%2C%20alongside%20their%20page%20numbers.

George, T. (2022). *Thesis & Dissertation Acknowledgements | Tips & Examples.* Retrieved from Scribbr: https://www.scribbr.com/dissertation/acknowledgements/#:~:text=The%20acknowledgements%20section%20is%20your,no%20longer%20than%20one%20page.

Hassan, H. (2022). Research Topics – Ideas and Examples. *Research Methods Network*, 1-14.

Indeed. (2022). *How to write a cover page (including cover page examples).* Retrieved from https://uk.indeed.com/career-advice/career-development/cover-page-example#:~:text=What%20is%20a%20cover%20page,sees%20upon%20receiving%20a%20work.

Kabir, M. (2018). Chapter 1. In *Introduction to Research* (pp. 1-24). Curtin University.

Madison. (2023). *Writing an Abstract for Your Research Paper.* Retrieved from The Writing Center, University of Wisconsin – Madison: https://writing.wisc.edu/handbook/assignments/writing-an-abstract-for-your-research-paper/

YOUR KNOWLEDGE HAS VALUE

- We will publish your bachelor's and
  master's thesis, essays and papers

- Your own eBook and book -
  sold worldwide in all relevant shops

- Earn money with each sale

Upload your text at www.GRIN.com
and publish for free